A Funny Thing Happened On The Way To Maturity

poems by

Wesley D. Sims

Cyberwit.net

HIG 45 Kaushambi Kunj, Kalindipuram

Allahabad - 211011 (U.P.) India

http://www.cyberwit.net

Tel: +(91) 9415091004

E-mail: info@cyberwit.net

Printed at Repro India Limited.

DEDICATION

To my father, Fagin Sims, who I credit with giving me my sense
of humor.

INTRODUCTION

Medical experts say laughing causes our bodies to produce endorphins, feel-good hormones.

One medical doctor says he laughs every day, even if he has nothing in particular to laugh about, just to get the benefits. We also know, *A merry heart doeth good like a medicine...*, Proverbs 17:22, KJV. My wish for you is that this book will engender the release of some happy hormones.

ACKNOWLEDGMENTS

Thanks to the editors of following publications in which the following poems first appeared in some form.

Time of Singing: " Coupon Clipper"

Plum Tree Tavern: "Choreographed Buzzards"

Parody: "Donations"

Pangolin Review: "Dictionary of Love"

Remember September Anthology: "Multi-Tasking "

Wordgathering: "Making New Friends"

The American Diversity Report: "Conversations with Cousins"

Paragon Review: "Shades of Gray, Tinge of Red"

Praxis Magazine: "Ode to the Irish Potato"

The Avocet: "Pretty Little Darlings", "Yard Work"

The Weekly Avocet: "Green"

Voices on the Wind: "If I Come Back"

BloodRoot: "Repair Work"

Magnets and Ladders: "Home Was a Swimming Hole"

Liquid Imagination Online: "Bare Bones Band"

Contents

Dictionary of Love

I

Love: Someone to whom you give a valentine.

Valentine: A card or thing given to a lover to elicit a smile.

Smile: A friendly stretched position of two lips.

Two lips: Pretty, romantic muscles that form a mouth.

Mouth: Anatomy for eating and exchanging kisses.

Kisses: Expression of love by sensual touching of two lips.

Tu-lips: Multicolored flowers that bloom in Spring.

Spring: A season for kindling romance by giving kisses and flowers.

Flowers: Plants with colorful petals you give to show love.

II

Octopus: Sea creature with many arms, but one mouth.

Mouth: Organ for eating and osculation.

Osculation: Omni-syllabled word for giving kisses.

Kisses: Special touching, hopefully not by an octopus, with two lips.

Lips: Muscular edges of a mouth used for osculation and eating octopus.

Bare Bones Band

Listen in the third watch of night when the moon
blares full and ghostly, in the little country graveyard
beside the spooky woods and you might hear a low
clacking sound as the Bare Bones Band comes to life.

Uncle Klem, that fiddling fool, emerges first, mildewed
instrument tucked under his ulna, drags his chalky wrist
along the bow to rosin it up then fiddles the fast notes
of *Cripple Creek.* The magical music draws Aunt Alma
out of her casket, and she sashays around the stones.
Roused by the vibrations, deaf Grandpa Gordy crawls
from his crusty chamber clutching his five string banjo,
dusts away dirt, begins to pluck the strings.
Cousin Carl and Sister Sallie climb up, plop down
and tap their drumstick toes on a tomb rock for rhythm.
In fifteen minutes a whole skeletal troop of cousins,
aunts, uncles, friends are fiddling, picking, clacking
and racking arms through do-si-do's among the namesake
markers. Silk flowers tremble as dust clouds bloom
a summer fog. They jamboree for hours, clicking
and clinking heels in the stony concert hall.

Their singing swings low, but if you listen hard,
if you can attune your ear to the dead, you might hear
the faint drum and hum of song until pre-dawn
begins to expose the moon-mellowed landscape.
And a little before twilight, they end the hoedown
and all file back down as Klem wraps it up sawing
on the standard, *When the Saints Go Marching In.*

Choreographed Buzzards

Aerial acrobatic show—
wake of turkey buzzards surf
the blue ocean of wind,
black bodies glistening, their silver
wing tips splashed by sunshine.
Like practiced dancers transitioning
through routines, they cycle up the cove,
shifting, changing patterns, congregated
first in a circle, followed by momentary
square, then a trapezoid, now a Dipper
constellation, followed by a dotted spline
that torques and bends into a question
mark, as if to ask—what is this?

Training run for young buzzards?
Some vulture-peculiar ritual
practiced in mating season?
A random drifting, sniffing,
sailing excursion over the lake?
Maybe it's just a Sunday afternoon
surfing flight, admiring the sites
and gawking at humans.

Downside Up

Looking to leverage his position
a little way up the ladder of success,
Uncle Sorbie scrounged a moonlighting
job, master of miscellany in a
lighting store. One day he ascended
the ladder to retrieve a prized selection.
Fixture half-detached, his arms raised
as if a sign of submission to the god
of supplemental income, his pants
surrendered, fell to kiss his feet.
The startled female patron repaired
the breach, held them up while
he backed down. Having slid
a few rungs back, his progress fizzled,
recovery crawled. She mended fast
but every time a full moon
climbed the sky she suffered
a sudden flashback.

Multi-Tasking

With quartz-time order the cosmos spins,
the planets ensconced in their cycles true,
the worlds of photons pulsing straight
along their paths. Then wander into the men's
room, discover chaos, your life taken
in your hands. Is light playing tricks
or the force field warped after
prestidigitation by multi-tasking hands?
Does Guinness record a demise
from asphyxiation induced by laughter?

I should have regarded the omen
last week, the rare alignment of five
planets all visible together, a string of white
pearls laced across the twinkling sky.
An amateur astronomer aimed my sight
with talented hands—*See them rise,
there and there.* I observed the jewels.

His mumbled response to the *Hi* I said
perturbed at once the fragile cup
of calm. A glance revealed the sudsed-up
pearls of bicuspids. Images whizzed by.
I saw again as a child an elder tease me
with the challenge to rub my head
and pat my belly simultaneously.

No cosmic arc here, a paler shade.
Standard hygiene, with his free

hand he brushed his teeth, while we
aligned leg to leg, no wall made
to separate the sparkling porcelain
fixtures turning our trajectories.

Making New Friends

No need to fret about making new
friends. Don't wait for some quake
to shake them to you or a hovering star
to spotlight one. Its easy as saying
"Howdy". Just be alert for opportunities,
don't obsess about flaws, failures
or awkward appearances. Think
loyalty and performance as gems
to value. For example, I made some
new ones on a hospital stay.
A kind nurse introduced us,
we spent some time together,
soon became inseparable.
They hung with me like buddies
through some trying times.
I shall always remember them,
my IV pole and catheter.

Conversation with Cousins

Cousin Mack from upstate Maine
snapped his syllables clean
and crisp like green beans
dropped in my grandmothers lap.
Jimmy Joe from Arkansas
plopped his words like handfuls
of new Irish potatoes
tossed into a bucket so we
missed the sound of some.
And cousin Marlow from Georgia
extruded his, pushed them out
like sausage, long fluid flow
with soft, squishy pauses
and periods held and strung out
so they seemed like dashes.

Ode to the Irish Potato

I like your tan and freckled skin,
your knobs, dimples, mysterious valleys.
Your eggish shape, pudginess don't repel me.
I know you wouldn't fracture like Humpty Dumpty
if you fell. No golden yolk to spill,
only delectable white flesh inside.
No matter where I stand,
your eyes are always waching me.
Your earthy aroma reminds me of fresh
turned soil, soft and loamy to my fingers.

Too loving, you turn soft in the hands
of all who embrace you,
but it's dicey to pursue you with passion,
for gravity holds it against me.

I feel my sentiments are sliced in two.
To keep or not to keep—
I dare not save you warm and moist,
lest you want to reproduce.
To eat or not to eat—my taste
buds delight in you,
but my appetite boils out of control.

They call you Irish, and I wonder
if it's the roots from which you grew,
or your intriguing eyes, or the questions you evoke:
(Is it true an Irishman answers a question with a question?).

Why so many eyes and dimples dear?
Why knobs, bumps, and little valleys to whet my curiosity?

How do I love thee? Shall I count some ways?
I love thee jacket on or off.
I love thee steamed and baked.
I love thee whole or diced.
I love thee fried and slightly brown.
And oh how I love thee creamed with butter.
I love thee to the breadth my waist can stretch.
And though they be cut short,
I shall love thee all the days of my life.

Green

Middle of May, my grandmother's
peony bushes had their lush blooms
of pink and purple, yellow and white.
They made sumptuous, colorful bouquets
for the house and the church piano.
Their strong aroma so memorable.
While the peonies were blooming
June apples were growing in the orchard,
eventually turning yellowish
or light green, with a slightly tart taste.
Just the thought of them tickles
the tongue. At age sixteen we'd ride
horseback under the tree and pick
some to eat Sunday afternoons.
But at age thirteen impatience
held sway. While visiting a friend
one day we ate too many too green,
learned a valuable lesson
about foods and colors.
Green kids, green judgment,
green faces, and a belly ache
to laugh about only when older
and imparting wisdom to children
and grandchildren.

Jumping A Stream

A full moon worked its magic.
Three teens in early spring
swallowed adventure like herons
gulping minnows. Trekked
cross country—hills, ditches, fences.
Searching snakes and snails,
whatever interesting creatures availed.

Stopped by a spillway behind the dam
of a ten acre lake. No need to walk
around, jumping is faster and more fun.
I leaped across, my buddy followed.
Then crash, splat, splash. His younger
brother tried but short legs betrayed him,
dished a cool weather baptism.
Not so funny to him, but thoughtless
humor slayed me. Did you know you
can pass out from laughter?

Donations

Queued to renew driver's license,
I spy some forms that plead donate
your organs, don't take them with you.
I consider how the mortician
will make chopped steak of them or burn
to dust to decorate some garden plot,
or scatter and make some mountain
or lake a couple pounds bigger.
I decide to get a leg up on immortality,
go green, join the recycle revolution,
implement piecemeal reincarnation.
I remember the old adage *Charity begins
at home*, so hereby make a plan
and will—donate some parts
to folks I know.

My right foreleg to Pegleg Pruitt
who donated his to a jungle in Viet Nam.
Two toes go to cousin Tom who blasted
his off with a shotgun propped on his foot.
My right hand I hand to classmate Karl
who shot his off to escape the draft.
Uncle Nehi gets a nod—both knees,
he wore his out begging Aunt Nancy
for forgiveness. My intestines ship
to neighbor Nabob who I heard Dad say
one time lacked the guts to stand up
to his bossy wife. My heart I hope shall
enliven Aunt Hilda who some folks

claimed never had one. My chin I will
to Uncle Charlie whose own so weak
atop a long neck, he looked like
a terrapin without the stripes.
My teeth shall be titled to cousin Tim
and tell his daughter Tina she won't
have to see her dad gum it anymore.
My bountiful nose I offer to neighbor
Norville who insulted mine so he can
know how it feels to walk a mile
with another man's schnooze.

My eyes please send to Grandpa George,
who often said he didn't "see into it"
about Social Security rules.
My bad ear I bequeath to Brother
Barney who would love a bona fide
excuse to listen to his gabby
Gertrude only half the time.
And finally, I bestow my brain,
wrinkled and lightly used,
to my buddy Billy Bob
whose teacher once declared
he didn't have one.

Shades of Gray, Tinge of Red

I gaze through the patio door,
its dulled aluminum framing the ocean.
My spouse lounges behind me,
face glued to a food magazine.
The sky grimaces in tones of gray.
Sea ripples in dark pewter.
Pale sand wallows in rain-drenched
drifts. Wave caps flicker gray-blue,
splash and fade on cloudy beach.

My eyes surf water's edge,
dotted with drab pastels of sweats
and tops. No neon T-shirts blaring,
no bold-colored brand name jackets.
I spy a young woman
strutting up the misty strand,
long hair fluttering in the breeze,
red bikini hugging curves.

My tan temples brighten,
tinge of red flushes my cheeks
when the familiar voice behind me
interrupts my daydream,
Penny for your thoughts.

Yard Work

Chickweed and sticks, always
litter my yard like permanent squatters.
I banish them and they come back
like buzzards flocking to a carcass.
Some hide in the grass and multiply
like rabbits and deer. The trees
drop limbs and branches
like my drill sergeant in basic training
always planting cigarette butts
at night (I concluded) so we would have
some to pick up the next day.
I'm constantly picking up and pulling,
hauling to the brush pile at woods edge
and the trash pile by the walnut tree.
And it too is a litter-ary agent, always
dropping leaves or limbs or walnuts.
When autumn comes the chickweed
slows and the leaves decide
to blizzard my lawn. Did I mention
squirrels? They're like a squad of statues
that get shuffled around every hour,
always scrounging nuts or burying nuts
or digging for nuts. My yard
is holy as a Mother Mary shrine.
All of it is driving me nuts.
I'm thinking of paving my lawn
and painting it green.

Pretty Little Darlings

Little darling greeted me
in the back yard, slender face,
dark eyes, coal black hair.
Seemed interested to meet me,
walked forward without hesitation.
I froze, unable to speak, not unlike
my bashful behavior at thirteen
in the presence finally of the attractive
classmate that peaked my blood pressure,
but so shy no words would pass my lips.

I retreated inside to ponder
the situation. Through the window
she seemed lost and lonely.
But then her sister appeared,
a twin, same exact features.
Courage up I went back out
where there was yet another sister.
Triplets? Oh, my. They all wanted
to meet me. Impressed but unsettled,
I stalled, equivocated in self-talk.

They surely seemed harmless, but
conditioning kicked in, triggered
a Pavlovian response.
The large, tell-tale white stripe
unnerved me. The lovely
little stinkers had no fear of me.
I spotted the mother loitering

close by at the edge of the yard.
Reasoned she would veto
any close relationship I might pursue.

Next day *five* little kits scrounged
around the yard. They visited
for several days, soliciting
food but I never obliged.
Like with some relatives,
it's good to see them come
but a greater joy to see them go.

Repair Work

Wait until the snarl of storm passes.
Tar won't stick to a wet roof,
and treading slippery slopes can be treacherous,
tricky as unguarded conversation
after your spouse has navigated
a hurricane of frustrations, disappointments.

Plan it first, make ready your mending kit.
Preparation can avoid a failed effort,
prevent a follow up session.
Timing is the linchpin of success.
When you're ready and the moment seems right,
approach the problem area with caution,
the place where a few irritating drops
surged into a record flood,
requiring fast mop up action,
precipitating reordering of priorities,
catapulting repair work to the top of your list.
Failure ensures you'll tiptoe through days
with tentative steps offering sweet apologies.

Home Was A Swimming Hole

*- and a fishing pole and the feel of a
muddy row between my toes.* — Joe Diffie

One was two miles west passing Mr. Harlan's
cattle ranch with the big, bad brahmas
with high back humps grazing in the pasture,
staring with mean faces and giant horns
you didn't even want to think about touching,
lest they butt you back into yesterday.
Travel the gravel road looping down
to Shoal Creek to where it curves to the bridge
then take the dogleg dirt road to the hole
deep enough to dive into from the jutting
limestone bluff. Water runs dingy but cools
a sweaty body. For sixeen year-olds that's enough.
If you stay all night and bring a long-handled
gig and good flashlight you can eat fried frog legs
for breakfast to go with the perch you catch.
You'll need a pot of strong coffee because you
stay up late swapping stories. Struggle
to get up early, ending the sweet dreams
about the hot classmates you'd like to date.
But you have to get in some more fishing,
hoping for a big mud cat or silver drum.

The other hole located two miles south,
past Grandma's house up and down hills
to the shallow, gravel-filled ford,
then a quarter mile south through

Mr. Belew's pasture, dodging cow patties
and avoiding the Jersey bull, then climb through
the barbed wire fence, drop your shorts and leap
into the ice cold stream of Blue Water Creek.
If you try to wade in you'll chicken out.
Just jump in and if you survive the shock
you can go for fifteen minutes provided
you swim like you just spied a cottonmouth.
After ten to fifteen minutes you hop out
and let the sun melt the icicles off your butt.
If you're really tough you dive back in
for a second round. By then you shiver
and shake trying to get your britches on.
By the time you ride your bike back home
you're all hot and sweaty again
but at least you have the memory
you can dredge up next time
the mercury hits ninety-five degrees,
and a story to tell your buddies and later
to your kids when they don't believe
you walked three miles to school every day
even in the snow.

Stopping in Town On a Snowy Evening

with apology to Robert Frost

Whose girl is that, face pure as snow?
For sure the daughter of Mitch Marlow,
but he won't mind me courting her,
especially if he doesn't know.

What is that angel doing here
with no boyfriend or father near?
Is this my chance, one I must take
or forever after cry in my beer?

She gives her long blond hair a shake
almost more than a guy can take,
those deep blue eyes, so soft and warm.
Was that a wink, did I mistake?

I'll hurry over, ply my charms,
get love's spring flowing, can do no harm.
But wait, there's my girl, Betty Jo.
She'll surely break my legs and arms.

I Found a Plum

Dark eyes and bangs drew accolades,
turned heads, and all my high school chums
admired her striking face and well-made
legs. I knew I'd found a plum.
I loved to nuzzle her cute nose,
stroke the curve of silk-soft ears.
She humored me, uncharmed I supposed,
not for love but out of fear.
Skittish and driven by desire
for protection, not much to inspire.
I strained to hold a firm grip,
ready to swivel at the hip.
One outing down a country road,
a flash, a pause, a bright thing glowed.
She jumped and turned a quick, cold shoulder,
whirled to run. I couldn't hold her,
was thrown and left to nurse a hurt,
prostrate, poised to kiss the dirt.
But when I thought, *What shall I do?*
I'm up the creek, without a paddle.
My filly's look said, *Man-up dude*
and jump back in the saddle.

Coupon Clipper

She clipped and saved
through all her life,
for rewards
pecuniary,

And I declare
she'll not expire
without a coupon
from the mortuary.

If I Come Back

Slaves of habit we humans,
susceptible to Pavlovian training.
I cant escape my raising.
The Thirties depression
scarred my dad's psyche.
Wouldn't hire a tradesman
for anything he could do.
But he had dexterity and talent,
nimble craftsman hands
could fix anything broken
from house to garage,
cars to tractors to machinery.
I can't stifle the tendency,
shutdown this maybe genetic
instinct to fix broken plumbing
and electrical gadgets.
I'm smart enough to do that.

I can curl or twist the wires,
screw them down, make loops
and neat embroidery of black
and white and red, and tape
them up like sutured wounds.
But the lights don't burn
and the fan won't turn,
or wires spark and breakers trip.
My big hands can cut and thread
or glue pipes but if the joints fit,
they leak, or hot goes to cold.

Patience runs thin as depression soup,
frustration breaks my resolve
to swear off swearing.
Working under the sink
I need instructions in Braille.
Arthritis in the neck and bifocals
insure I can't contort my body
to get under there and see
at the same time.
I have to work by feeling.

If reincarnation is real,
bring me back
as a plumber/electrician
so I can flush all that frustration
down a well-lit drain.

Focus Said The Muse

with admiration for Poe's *The Raven*

Once upon an evening weary
writer's block and very bleary-
eyed. I had my pencil tapping,
tapping on my writing pad.
Suddenly there came a rapping,
rapping sound that made me glad.

Muse came speaking at my door,
You'll be writing evermore.
Focus, she said, On your task
when I am or am not nigh.
To help your project I just ask
write some words even if you're dry
every day at appointed time,
you show up, I'm right behind.

Lunch

Occasionally I have for lunch
a luscious plate of spaghetti,
stirring those long, skinny noodles
slithering around in a lather
of reddish, spicy sauce underneath
a mound of soft, brown meat-balls.
How those slick noodles slide in
your mouth and right down
your throat if you're not careful.
These tasty little ropes make
the stomach sing with happiness.

Sometimes when dining
on this delectable dish
I think back to the time
of my youth when one day
at the little country store
I joined two playmates in dire need
not so much for nourishment
as for a serving of excitement.
Big brother offered little brother
an incentive, a nickel if he'd eat
just one wiggly earthworm
and he did.

About the Author

Wesley D. Sims has published three chapbooks of poetry: *When Night Comes*, Finishing Line Press, Georgetown, Kentucky, 2013; *Taste of Change*, Iris Press, Oak Ridge, TN, 2019; and <u>A</u> *Pocketful of Little Poems*, Amazon, 2020.

He has had poems nominated for Best of the Net and the Pushcart Prize.

His work has appeared in *Artemis Journal*, *Bewildering Stories*, *Connecticut Review*, *G.W. Review*, *Liquid Imagination*, *Novelty Magazine*, *Pine Mountain Sand and Gravel*, *Plum Tree Tavern*, *Poem*, *Poetry Quarterly*, *Proverse*, *Quill & Parchment*, *The American Diversity Report*, *The South Carolina Review*, *Time of Singing*, *Word Gathering*, and several other journals and anthologies.

www.ingramcontent.com/pod-product-compliance
Lightning Source LLC
Chambersburg PA
CBHW051830130726

47987CB00003B/1487